# We Are...
## A Bundle of Feelings and Emotions

Poems by

Susan Lidia Montes De Aragon

A publication of

Eber & Wein Publishing

Pennsylvania

We Are…
A Bundle of Feelings and Emotions
Copyright © 2022 by Susan Lidia Montes De Aragon

All rights reserved under the International and Pan-American copyright conventions. No part of this book may be reproduced, stored in a retrieval system, or transmitted in any form, electronic, mechanical, or by other means, without written permission of the author.

Library of Congress
Cataloging in Publication Data

ISBN 978-1-60880-706-2

Proudly manufactured in the United States of America by

# Eber & Wein Publishing

Pennsylvania

To my family:

Through the written word, we can perceive and understand the
true self of a person and discover what is hiding within the soul.
In these pages you are going to find a handful of feelings and
emotions that moved me throughout my life…


To my dear friends:

I close my eyes in an effort to extend myself into the future,
The future that awaits either like a black hole wet in tears
Or like a white, beautiful dove, waiting to be held in our hands…
And the likeness that makes our friendship so dear,
Is the certainty of not knowing whether it will be you or I
(The fortunate to hold finally a white dove.)
Let's hope that, in our close or separate destinies,
They will be two, one for each one of us…

Because to me:

Poem is floating in the air, in the colorful spring, in a storm among the rain, in the winter with the fog.

Poem can be in the hearts of anyone: the cruel, the sad, the good, the bad.

Poem comes with a flower, in a wound, with a kiss, with a tear;

It can be sometimes a confession, a piece of paper in which we reveal our most dear secrets,

It can be a treasure of happiness or the cry of a desperate heart…

But whatever it reveals, poem is always hiding deep in the hearts of everyone…

*We Are...A Bundle of Feelings and Emotions*

## Me

I am leaving behind the scratch of a pen
In a white empty page
That means something
Or has nothing to say…

And I am moving like a butterfly,
To and fro,
For whom nobody cares
And nobody knows…

Here I am today,
Tomorrow just dust that the wind blows.
But my soul persists,
Its essence to be known.

You did not know me.
But my fragrance will linger on,
And you will find me here,
After the curtain falls in a sudden dawn…

## We Are

We are now here, like a grain of sand
That a wave has deposited on shore from a green sea of life…

We are living in a little flame that moves to and fro,
Sometimes high and sometimes low, in a candle light…

And, in every turn of the traveling wind,
We are moved here and there, like a helpless leaf…

We are moving forward in the extended wings of a butterfly
Searching for the nectar of flowers in an open field…

And we tinkle in laughter, like a bell, in the rays of the sun
And shed a tear, like the dew of flowers in dawn, in the darkest night…

We are like the classical notes of a song that we created alone,
Sounding loud or in a quiet tone, until it dies,
And is heard maybe again someday, maybe no more…

We aspire to leave, like a scar on earth,
An elephant footprint for the future to see.

Just because, when we are here,
We like to plant an eternal seed…

## A Second Chance

As a child, I found my soul traveling in a rapid flight among the fields,
Between green mats and vivid red earth,
Underneath a clear blue sky
And cotton clouds…
And, even though I died, I had a second chance
To take again a breath
Of a new life…
It was a peaceful and quiet rest
After the turmoil and struggle of my path.
Traveling thru a tunnel, among nature,
Until my soul stopped in front of two angels;
There was a sweet, low voice, that asked me:
"What do you want?"
I answered: "I want my mommy."
And the angel told the other angel,
And their voices died among the whistling
Of the rushing wind.
And I opened my eyes…
It was the wish of God
To grant me again the miracle of life…

*Susan Lidia Montes De Aragon*

## Here We Are

And here we are,
Like little butterflies flying among the plants,
Stopping briefly for the nectar of flowers,
Rapidly moving our wings as we go around and around.
And the birds sing as we dance and dance
A melody of love and life…

## Life

Life is the feeling of existence,
It is time measured through space till death,
It is a story to sometimes end
In some obscure day,
                      So is life to men.

It is fire growing weak
Until a tiny blow of wind blows it out,
And it is in our hearts a beat
To exist.
                      So is life to men.

A limited time for us to exist.
A continued path that it we chose to be,
A past so made, a future planned
That we so dreamed…
                      So is life to me…

*Susan Lidia Montes De Aragon*

## Work

Sometimes our hard search for dreams
Leaves us in ways;
That we think ahead waits for us
A hopeless road;
But whatever we work hard
To build today
We will find tomorrow
As life moves along.
Because if we plant on earth
Something will grow
And if we care for flowers
Our roses will bloom...

## The Leaves

The Autumn wind roughly touches the leaves of the trees,
And soon the leaves will fall to the wind,
Like dead bodies they let themselves be pushed;
To somewhere, to someplace, to somewhere they move…
And like Autumn winds move away the leaves from the trees,
And exhausted, slowly they fall on earth, lifeless things;
Also hopes of man are pushed away by the winter air
To suddenly dry the heart from breath, from faith.
And the leaves, rolling, to somewhere they go.
But the hopes of man, to nothingness fall…

*Susan Lidia Montes De Aragon*

Loneliness

Loneliness is to be somebody and feel nobody.
It's to walk thru roads of life like a ghost.
To move like a shadow of a man, without the man;
To be like a leaf, which from a tree the wind has blown…

Loneliness is a feeling of emptiness,
It's to know you are there but not what for;
It's to speak, and to think the spoken word
A thousand times, and maybe more…

To feel death?...Men do not know,
Could ever it be to be alone?...
To feel death, only God knows,
Men only fears to be alone…

## Search

The truth I found… and now, I'm searching for a Trace of Light
Among the shadows of reality…
Just think, that "All" so soon to die,
And yet, ignoring how to feel "Alive."

I fear a meaningless, unlighted road,
The loneliness of a moonless night…
I fear to have a dreamless sleep
Until the end of a dull path…

I fear that upon awakening in the middle of a night
I'll find no one for my dreams to touch;
To fall alone among shadows, sure to come,
And there'll be no hope for my heart to grasp…

I place a wondered look on present trends;
What of myself in days waiting to come?
I was leaning hard on crushed beds
Of dreams, that broken, had passed…

I'll know…and all "soon," I hope,
The moon will light me to my marked road…

*Susan Lidia Montes De Aragon*

## USA

My parents brought me to this country and I was eager to find
A brotherly embrace, a welcomed smile;
To work on this earth till my fruits ripe;
To mix…to belong…to give birth…to die…

Because life is a cocktail of emotions;
A handful of hopes, a cup of despair, a rainbow of laughter;
The beating of time, and then, the all peaceful silence.
No matter the country, no matter the color…

## I Am

What I am I think
And I think as I am,
So, how to search for a new me
If only the old myself is what I found?

How to measure insights
If I am to think and myself to judge…?
And because I am like all
I forget my faults and defend my rights…

*Susan Lidia Montes De Aragon*

People

People are funny, but false to themselves,
Here and there of marriage complain;
Their troubles and sorrows to friends they confess.
But when they encounter an acquaintance of theirs,
And the acquaintance tells them the problem he faces,
The "champions" answer proudly: "of us you should learn,
Don't be so ungrateful, your tears please forget…"
"Don't be so complaintful of all that is bad,
You should be so happy with that…that you have…"

## The Giant

<u>Martin Luther King</u>, a giant of a man,
Soft and kind his soul like a tender, warm hand,
Extended to give compassion and help to any heart;
But strong like iron, his spirit, shed light
Throughout the mind of men of this misleaded land.

<u>Martin Luther King</u> ideals were surely inspired by god,
For also God asks always for kindness and respect for All
and every One.
<u>Martin Luther King</u>, a good american
His efforts were to make, among men, a strong and united bond.

His sacrifice was not in vain.
His words, wise and sharp, were like a sword
That finally broke his brothers chains…
His deed left a creative, inspiring tale
For the tender souls of youngster of the past and following days.

<u>Martin Luther King</u>, you inspired admiration;
And I learn from you, sir, with respect and veneration.
You will always be remembered in all our hearts
Because you shaped the history of this nation…

Great ideals of a golden heart
That enriched the actions of this great man.
His mind empowered by the word of God
And his spirit molded by His hands…

*Susan Lidia Montes De Aragon*

## Human Soul

I move, I move through space,
And there is the constant beat of time, so infinite,
And, thru it, I live.
I eat, I sleep, I dream all thru the night, to survive.
I talk, I love, I cry and hate, to exist…

To time, to space, what is my life worth?
Is it a minute portion in matter?
Is it oxygen that so many times I steal from air?
Or, is it a little body more, to that manner?

Whatever it is to me it doesn't matter.
God knows, and I, like any other man, do know:
That precious are all those human souls
That try to improve each day a little more…

## War

All torches of night were torches of war,
And torches of life went down,
And nights were the thunder of thousand of skies
Beating the earth, crushing all life…

Night took over all shape of the town,
And death quiet prayers and cries.
Lights of anger explode one by one,
Shaking the walls, rests, and hearts…

And then…there was silence and cold.
No noise, no lights, but a deathly smell
And the lifeless shells of men
                            All on earth…

*Susan Lidia Montes De Aragon*

War

So many young men fall,
So many young men are gone…
Buds, that crushed, withered,
Blown in the fury of stories untold.
Lights fading away
In the dawn of a day…

We, in the city, try to be civilized,
But, oh, jungle of war, it has to be wild,
And we bury deep our feelings
In this senseless fight
To survive…to survive…

Oh God, oh God, there is no end
For the fate of men again to be bend.
Please give us peace again
For love to be spread
On the surface of earth…

So that, united, we might march
In every country, hand in hand.
To offer the love that we have learned
From the teachings of God…

Prayer of war

And then, when Earth is Earth again,
When Hell is buried far below,
And above is paradise offering love,
Let's hope that God will care
And make the home of men,
                    The home of peace…

*Susan Lidia Montes De Aragon*

## If

If I could let myself be carried away by a note of a soft symphony
Or touch perfection with my lips and let its velvet petals fall in my heart.
If I could fly away like the clouds pushed by the mighty wind,
And slowly melt, become invisible, intermingled with nature's parts…

I would like to touch with magic hands those cold hearts iced with prejudice,
To see all races mixing together, and see white, black, brown, and yellow walk hand in hand…
If I could hear above a sound and see beyond a sight…
Then, I could see and hear clearly the soul of men,
And I would like to break such habits that make this world starve a child…

If I could walk among the crowds and paint a smile in every face,
And, like the sun, evaporate the tears that bring forth our pain…
Like almighty, good and godly, burst like a bubble in laughter
And make a miracle: to all people give happiness…

Then, I would see the hate of men fading away,
And I could wipe all tears from a child's face.
Cleanse all hypocrisy from all embrace,
And walk away, walk away from this sadness and despair…

Nature

While little flowers at her feet are at rest,
Those roses, gardenias, camellias,
Are blossoming perfections, here and there,
Filling the air with all their scents.
I am holding a rose of red petals painted,
And, looking it, I'm moved, it is created so perfectly.
It's delicate perfume reached my soul and my heart was taken…
Time passed and today, soon is tomorrow for us,
And outside, is nature, unbelievable, untouched,
To give us memories and beauty unmatched,
To give us peace and our spirits touch,
To give us new hope and fill us with love…

*Susan Lidia Montes De Aragon*

## My Heart

You give me comfort, you give me peace;
Help me endure the turmoil of my life.
You charge my body with the strength I need
To help me, day by day, get by…

And, after every lovely moment that we spent,
You stop, to ask me how I feel,
Bath in the wonderful pleasure of your warm embrace
My heart silent prefers to be…
(I cannot answer you
What I cannot find within me…)

It's really hard to comprehend:
We dream of love to come our way,
And yet we choose to reject
When someone offers it to us some day…

My heart: "What is it that you want?"
You cannot live of dreams of passions that have died…
Time is passing… "Aren't you afraid to be condemn
To a sad and lonely life?"

## Is It I?

Dear…when you wake up in the morning,
Or when you come back to a silent house.
When you are ready to go to bed
And you relax, close your eyes,
Who comes to your mind?
Is it I?

And dear…when you are far away
And many days passed by;
And you are all alone
In quiet invitation to fantasize.
Who is it with?
Is it I?

Because if you don't feel any desire
To feel me close and embrace me tight,
To hear my voice,
To keep in touch.
Then, I am not the one…

Because…
With your smile you bring the joy
In which I drown all my sorrows,
And
It will bring a smile to me
As I remember it in all my tomorrows…

*Susan Lidia Montes De Aragon*

## My Candlelight

Like a little ballerina in a music box,
I dance around, around
Until the box is closed
And the music stops…
I have no feelings
My heart relaxed;
My feet following
The happy rhythms of all the sounds…
And my body moves and moves
To the music of the band…
Meanwhile, my soul,
Waiting to be touched,
Awaits,
In painful loneliness lies…
Wondering whether there's anyone
With a magic wand,
Offering the tender love
To make my heart become alive,
Before the wind blows away
My fading candlelight…

## Love

Nothing matters, if I could grasp
A moment of this magic I call "love,"
And experience the tenderness in the embrace of your arms
That fills with wonderful warmth my empty heart…

And, in any instance of our lives,
If we can just experience a second of pure delight.
Our tender lips bond together, our bodies tenderly intertwined,
With that special soulmate we think we love.

A picture engraved forever in our hearts
To recollect many tomorrows of our lives,
And bring a smile in a nostalgic face,
And sweet memories in any lonely night…

"So, close your eyes my only one,
And let us enjoy this present moment
Before it's past…"

*Susan Lidia Montes De Aragon*

A Lesson

And with a tear rolling off my cheek
A sharp pain in my romantic soul
You were the love that filled my heart
And brought to me the rebirth of that joy…

There's a lesson in your future
There's a lot to learn yet;
For happiness cannot be bought
In any instant of life.
It's only a mystery that's still untold
In the spiritual satisfaction of a heart
And that cannot be obtain with gold
But only found by godly chance
In one of those fortunate turns of our lives…

# He

He did not call…
Like a leaf falling into my path
That from a dry, old tree had fall,
He came suddenly into my life…
It was an abrupt awakening of my romantic dreams;
A creeping trembling and unexpected feeling in my heart.
He did not follow or desire my crazy, unfounded wish;
He did not even keep the memory of our meeting in mind.
I know…because he did not call…
He wants to move me away into his past,
Like a little shadow
Of a dove passing in flight.
Because his wish to see me is just a little narrow
Arrow entering, as he desires, into his mind.
I have to erase his deceptive image from my dreams
And to these stupid notions say: goodbye!

*Susan Lidia Montes De Aragon*

It's Only Me!

My life is a stormy sea of emotions
Devouring all energy from my mind.
After our only meeting, I have to bury all feelings
That you woke up in my heart…

You're not to be blamed, it's only me,
It's only my need to love and be loved
That is eager to fill my heart
With foolish dreams…

And I call God to ask again
For all His help:
To forever forget you
And love forget….

(This was but a petal falling in my lonely heart
And now is like a knife cutting my soul in pieces.
Another sad failure, a nightmare on my mind,
I want to change, feel nothing, a cold stone become
And only laugh to emotion until I die, not cry…)

## Hi Emptiness

I was still feeling your heart warming my heart,
The pressure of your arms in your embrace,
The tender memory of the night you made love to me
Before you left…

It's hard to grasp that all that
Was the imagination of my mind, in all its crave
For an instant of love,
That wasn't there…

So, as you wish,
Goodbye, my love,
Hi emptiness…

*Susan Lidia Montes De Aragon*

To Peter

(What can it be?...You said you care for me
But, when I'm with you, you seemed so far away...)

I was searching carefully for a sparkle in your eyes
In the emotionless expression of your face,
I was just looking for a sign of love
A warm gesture to light up my heart...

It was so obvious, there was no connection,
When, next to me, you tried to attract the attention
Of any other attractive lady passing by
In order to add more to your mental treasures...

And, in my presence, it was such a humiliation
To see you adding another woman's number to your collection.
You said you love me...
(It must be another of your mind's inventions.)

What are you looking for?
Another fool that can believe in you
After so many deceptions?

You asked me if you are the one I'm searching for,
Are you the man that cares for me (and me alone)?
Or are you still looking (even when you're with me),
For someone else to come along?

## Better Alone

We are not going to mention how "I am,"
I'm not going to say a word about how "you are."
We are just going to accept that, in the time we spent,
We realize that, although my destiny crossed your path,
We have to continue alone and on our way.
We were both lonely, anxious to love,
A little bit impulsive in our search,
Without thinking, in a moment of passion,
We let it take me away and into your arms,
And I surrendered completely to give you "myself"
It was wrong, too soon to know
If we can respond to the needs of our souls in their quest.
My words in anger made you fall,
Your words alarmed my heart, made me depressed.
It's always better to be alone
Than to be with someone that doesn't bring forth the best
And bring us the happiness that we had lost…

*Susan Lidia Montes De Aragon*

## No Escape

You chose to send me a paper
In which you chose to brake this tie.
Then, why calling me,
Why ask me why?
Just do what it's expected;
What follow it's "goodbye!"

You chose to pick up pieces;
You chose to go away…
I chose to solve my problem
From which there is no escape.
Your destiny is to travel and be happy,
My destiny is to fight and stay…

Two opposites roads that's never meeting.
And always will run their ways…
You chose to lose me over lust;
Love to you is but a game.
You win a heart and toss it aside
If there is no material gain.

You think that love can be bought,
But love cannot be obtained.
You cannot price it for all the gold.
There is no measure for this treasure you lost…

## Be Advised

Because, my friend, please be advised:
Be good to the woman that you love.
For her tender, sweet words can change to a sad goodbye.
For every slap of yours to her heart
Has closed a door to be the one
To lead her soul into your life,
And although there are many buds hiding in green hills,
You'll never get this flower back…

*Susan Lidia Montes De Aragon*

## Sparks of Dreams That Have Not Died

Come…come see into my eyes,
Inside them, those lights,
Sparks of dreams that have not died,
And, although years have passed me by,
The well of love has not yet dried,
And hope to find love again drives on my life…

Come…come see into my eyes,
Can you perceive in them a melancholic sight?
All the loneliness that a smile cannot hide,
And, far, a sight can only catch the invisible one that loves me
And I cannot find…

And, all there are, are men that like to hold my hand;
Dancing around, around,
Are actors, puppets, imitators,
That act like if they are in love
But wish to hide from me their hearts….

# Hope

After so much struggle to survive,
Life left me empty.
Like a doll with a smiling mask, trying to leave behind
All the painful peddles in my past...
Still carrying deep, inside my heart,
An inch of hope, for the happiness that I'm so eager for
And I cannot find...
Where are you?
My little branch to save me
In the furious river of destiny, my life.
Who are you?...Or what are you?
Something I'm expecting to find in my continuous path,
And is hiding from me.
Am I going to find you before I die?
At night, dreams are always lightening
A little candle of expectations within my heart.

*Susan Lidia Montes De Aragon*

Invisible Love

There is a hole in my heart
That awaits to be filled with your love…
My hands extended
Yearning for the warmth of your loving touch…

My lips were sealed with empty kisses of lovers
I had,
Who only offered me passion,
And filled me with foolish, romantic dreams that, broken, died…

I feel like a little, cotton seed,
Floating softly at the mercy of the playful wind,
Waiting to fall into the bed of the land
To finally grow, and its roots set free…

I feel like a lost, little butterfly,
Moving rapidly its winds in her searching flight
For the soothing, sweet nectar in every flower
Of colorful, green plants…

Where can I find you
To stay and share this short road of my life,
Am I going to meet you before my last breath
Darkens this flame that my hope lights?

## Wrong!

If you just knew what is within,
The body always carry the spirit very deep…

If you just knew but wants to ignore
What's bury in my soul
Because the truth you don't admit…

If you want to see ME wrong you will persist.
THAT which is NOT there you'll see,
And you will always be lost
Blind, in a path of uncertainty…

Because, regarding ME
You have to remove from your eyes the deceitful veil
To clearly SEE…

*Susan Lidia Montes De Aragon*

## Brake the Chain

I feel numb, no feeling comes to my heart.
All I want is to brake the chain of this marriage
Which is holding me in lonely slavery.
He told me he no longer needed my "services,"
He had "somebody else" on the side;
That he would come home at any time:
3:00 A.M., 4:00 A.M., as always…
All I was thinking of, was the boys,
I told him so.
The boys are old enough to be aware,
That it was wrong for dad to come so late,
And they were hurt…
I don't feel anything any more.
All I think of is about the future of my sons.
My mind is about to explode,
Thinking how to right this horrible wrong
That is destroying our lives…
"Please God, light my path…"

## The Most

There is a spot that stains my glass.
And erase it, I tried, but it still grows.
Clouds in my life making my soul
Fall in pain each day a little more…

I see my desires like little bubbles of soap
Floating away and up into the air.
Those are my hopes
Bursting in to the open space, to nothingness…

But in the mist of it ALL;
Of all I WAS and still COULD BE.
There must be a trace of strength to fight left in the mold
With all my might and for all my dreams.

For <u>I'M NOT GIVING UP</u> and you should know
We should <u>ALL</u> try to the end: <u>TO BE</u>
<u>WHAT WE WISH TO BE THE MOST</u>…

*Susan Lidia Montes De Aragon*

Flowers of the Field

Look at the many flowers of the fields
Opening to expose colorful petals in their picturesque awake;
Awaiting the gentle fondling of the passing wind;
The rays of the morning sun in its warm embrace…

Those are like our children in their wonder world
With their little hands extended searching for a guiding light;
And we are here to nourish their inquisite minds
To provide a ladder for them, a path to find…

We are teachers, counselors, a second home for them.
We are a bridge leading them to where they want to get.
We offer them a "ear" because we try to be their "confidant,"
A "voice" because we try to comprehend what they say…

And look at our children, everyone with a luminous happy face.
They want us to hold their hand;
To surround their minds in an exciting embrace,
To cultivate and nourish their lives…

A time of their lives engraved forever in their hearts when they graduate
And, as they are walking forward to their next goal and, from us, away,
To come back, triumphant, in the future, to say
"Hello and thank you"…someday…

## The Children

In a half lost world
Of crazy symphonies untold,
Of violence and despair,
Of poverty and unjust wrongs,
We like to stretch our arms to grasp
The extended little hands
Of all the children.
Like small branches of a tree
That are trying to reach the sky
Searching for answers and direction in every cloud
To guide their tender lives…

We are the receiving ships
Taking them, one by one,
To the welcoming ports
Of their wondering minds;
Trying in every turn
To bring them closer to the "light"
With the tools
That only knowledge provides…

And we see them growing like little seeds we plant in a garden
So their flowers, some day, can our world delight.
Every word and gesture in their pathway into their eager mind engraved
Looking for a flashlight for their roads to light.

We are here, to discipline, educate,
To take them by their hands
Give them a safe map for their future to guide.

And we see our students in the future,
As successful men and women coming back,
In a nostalgic trip into their past

*Susan Lidia Montes De Aragon*

Pupils

If we can feed
A grain of aspiration
Into their hungry, eager minds.
To carry over to future generations
All lessons they can take from us.
Then a little inch of accomplished satisfaction
Is more regarding than a mile of worldly admiration.
For YOURS is the world that we supply you;
And OURS is the reward of your success in future steps of our nation…

## Our Children

What are children?
But a continuation of our own life.
An important ideology to describe
What is known as "eternity."
Because our fruits keep within their bodies
A part of our inner-selves
To continue our existence
Even after our own death,
And to spread our own genetic being
Throughout more and more tomorrows.

*Susan Lidia Montes De Aragon*

## To My Offsprings: Buds of My Life

And the stories of lying, malicious voices told,
Can change the characters of anyone.
Can distort the image on the mold,
And if you don't catch the essence of my being,
For it is what it is, as it comes,
It is what my creator gave me as a gift.
And if you cannot see it,
If you cannot my soul perceive,
You will miss what I can give you:
The wish of goodness for you is: in me.
My hands extended can give you all the love
That my soul holds only for you: to receive…
Now, if you don't welcome it…it will be lost
In a sea of pain…forever gone…
When the breath of life my body leaves…

*We Are...A Bundle of Feelings and Emotions*

A Mystery…

What is behind Prince Ethan Smile?
Are there angels in his sleep
Giving him so much delight
That his happiness he cannot hide?
Maybe remembrances of happy moments
From All his Past Lives.
(If I could solve the Mystery)
Yes, I would like to shrink
And be a butterfly
To sweetly touch his baby face
And fill him with so much love
That, in his cheerfulness,
I will tickle continuously his tiny heart
And stamp forever in his little face
A wonderful, eternal smile…

Grandbaby: give me your hand,
I will hold you and guide you
To the best road possible in your life.
Because your smile will always be
Like a bud opening, within me,
To fill with Tender Happiness my heart…

*Susan Lidia Montes De Aragon*

To Norma:

This is a beautiful dove that flew away;
She gently moves her wings toward the sky…
She is leaving behind castles of love that she made
With her kind gestures in our hearts…
Friends are not leaves that, with the wind, passed by;
They are always around us with a helping hand.
Friends do not criticize, they understand,
And paint in our faces a great smile…
Norma, her memory will always be in our minds,
Because her presence brought happiness to our hearts.
When friendship is perfect, it never ends:
Our loving friend, in Heaven, will wait for us…

*I dedicate this poem to Norma Ficarra for the many years of affection and friendship that she and her husband Vicente shared with my parents, Artemio and Pilar Montes. I always admired their generosity and kindness; they are an inspiration to me.*

Words

Words can leave forever a trace,
Like the drops of rain that fall
In the soft, warm sand of the ocean's shore, to remain…
And they cause pain, because mean words
Can eternally wound the heart
Like a painful sword…

Remember: Words stay recorded in the inner folds of our minds,
And what's easily said can hardly be erased.
Words stay inside
To be remembered over and over again
All our lives…
That's why when a word is said,
It is always better if IT is NICE….

*Susan Lidia Montes De Aragon*

The Power of Words

Be careful with the words you utter.
They can place a "nobody" in a pedestal
Or a "king" in the gutter…

Words have the power to lift your spirit to touch the clouds
Or torture your ego and make it crash.
Because words can humiliate you and bury your mind into the mud
Or transport you with them into a beautiful paradise…

Don't ever underestimate the power of your words.
Always remember: they are the ones that make history in the world…

Words can make a bad impression so people can put you down
Or make you look so good everybody wants to keep you on their side…

So, be careful, when you utter a word;
Remember: all the lives they touch and spirits they mold…

## To Dede

Walking among this new path
I was profoundly hurt.
For no reason, I was attacked
By impatient words,
And insulting eyes
From twisted souls
Whose only faults are to be blind.
But, among them all
There was you, friend,
And with a smile
You threw my way
A rose…
For the salvation of my mind…

Thank you.

*Susan Lidia Montes De Aragon*

In This Corrupted Times

I close my eyes because I like to see,
Within me,
All virtues that I left behind in order to co-exist
In this corrupted times…

I close my mind to work,
Because I like to reason the truths
That die in the deceit of fouls
In other liar's lies

And because I value all integrity,
I would like to close my heart to this black world;
So that, intact my sincere soul,
Would not be touch, slammered, and hurt…

## Wrong

In my despair I asked for help to many men;
And, once more, I sin in acting wrong.
The only one that can answer my call is God;
For He is the only one that knows it all…

And after falling in wrong a thousand times,
I choose my destiny, to meditate alone,
To chew in anger frustrations of my soul
And to cry again, and in the future more…

*Susan Lidia Montes De Aragon*

Ted's Prayer

Walking among the fields in the open space
I feel some hope coming my way;
But, evil lies hidden in words,
Told me to follow his lost soul
Of riches that I craved to have,
And in an unfortunate turn of life, I later lost…
Please God, forgive me…
I stumbled then, and then the fall.
Please let a little light come thru this crack,
Among the shadows of this frightful night,
To be always at your side
Till the end of this,
My futile life…

## Help

Within me, deep, a voice is begging help.
In silent whisper I ask for You, my Lord,
Because tormented by walls of crashing faith,
I see, within me, the dying of my soul…

Oh please, my God, don't let my heart because of his despair
Within the pit of vengeance and meanness fall.
Let me be clean, so that free of ugly thoughts
My being would survive in the perishing of this world…

*Susan Lidia Montes De Aragon*

## To My Cousin Nidia

Her hand extended like a magic wand
Is trying to reach the loving hearts
Of those to whom she wish to bring
A smile…

She tries too hard and sometimes not knowing how
To solve the problems among loved ones;
A hidden desire to bring justice and happiness
To everyone…

With a generous gesture,
She tries to bring back
The happiness that she got
From loved ones in her childhood past…

"Nobody's perfect" but with due respect
She planted many flowers in the field
That she deserves to collect.

She, my cousin Nidia, has shown evidence
Of a tender, kind heart,
And, in every step she takes in her rightful path,
She's building treasures
That enriches her and our spirit in life…

*We Are...A Bundle of Feelings and Emotions*

What I Would Like:

Wouldn't it be nice to be a butterfly,
And move my wings
To fly toward the open sky?
To feel free moving into the blue abyss,
And float peacefully among the white clouds…

Wouldn't it be nice to be myself?
No cage, no ropes, to hold my life,
Feel free from this, my destiny,
To be finally me, and live for myself
For what I want,
Without anything holding me…

My spirit is dying and it wants to survive.
Without freedom to be myself
There is no life….

*Susan Lidia Montes De Aragon*

Close the Door

And the best time of all,
Is when I go inside my room, and close the door.
I put a tape in my mouth,
Cover my ears,
And close in a chamber my soul
So it will not suffer anymore,
Exposed to betrayals and lies
Of all this world that never care for me…
And I am giving up;
I will not cry, no tears, no more…
And I'll be like a leaf rolling in the wind
Until it's bury in a dusty road.
Like an invisible heart
That was, and soon to disappear:
Today here…tomorrow gone…
Let the track of my steps, that I left behind,
Be bury in the sand in a wild storm,
And I will ask God to let a plant grow
From the inside of my being
To adorn with flowers a mountain top.
That's the only thing that I like to leave
At the end of my destiny
When God will call…

## Bad Times

I keep trying to see ahead in future times,
What to become of me, of us…
Just like a weed creeping thru the grass,
Bad luck took us by surprise.

My soul, frustrated, so many times, quit feeling,
And now, like a puppet, moves numb.
Tired, I'm walking in shadows,
Wondering how long bad times are going to last…

Sadness overtake me, whenever my children
Lose sight of the truth,
And with fiery eyes and insulting words
Forget I'm their mother, the root
From which their lives grow…

I dream so of a family united,
A true bed of love and peace,
A place where we can drown the suffering
That hardship on life can bring…

Oh God, I pray so for wonderful wisdom.
Maybe, if so, I may find an answer, a way
To save whatever is left in our little kingdom,
To find tranquility now on, from this day…

*Susan Lidia Montes De Aragon*

## This Yellow Fluid

This yellow fluid that numbs my brain,
And burns my throat,
Makes me forget what hurts,
And erases all painful thoughts
That bothers me, and lingers on
In my unrestful soul…

This yellow fluid that makes me dizzy,
And takes me to an endless maze;
Lost in a sea of nothingness
In which there is no pain…
Floating in a cloud of cotton, motionless…
An illusive, momentary protection from all despair…

But, I know this magic drink
Cannot bring me the peace
To live as my soul desires,
To satisfy my deepest wish…

## Pain

They say we must pay
For our bad deeds in our past lives.
I must of caused a lot of pain
To everyone that my destiny had touched
Because my struggle continues every day,
Doesn't end with the passing of the night.

If every tear I shed
Could be converted to bread,
All the world I would fed.
Please take away the darkness
That invaded our lives,
When the eyes of demons
Play with the innocence of our hearts.
When is justice going to be done?

When am I going to find God in my path
To give me the peace I am searching for,
And take me slowly into the light
To rest and suffer pain no more?

*Susan Lidia Montes De Aragon*

In These Pandemic Times

Look at the infinite Horizon,
Roads of Hope closing in these Pandemic Times.
A black, mortal shadow turning off lives' lights,
And I perceive the Hand of God
Picking my brothers' souls, one by one…
Within the walls in Victim's isolation
Their sickly bodies wait for more signs of the virus invasion.
Time to dig into their spirit, engaged in Sacred Meditation:
"Are they going to be Saved, or passed away,
Waiting for an anticipated Revelation…?"
My heart is aching throughout this march.
I pray for YOU tonight
And tomorrow more and more of YOU, to add,
For Parents, Brothers and Sisters
For Sons, Daughters, and Grandchildren…
And in my being, deep inside,
A voice incites me to talk to everyone around:
"Brothers and sisters:
Give me your hands and hold on very tight,
I know this nightmare will pass us by…
This is only a Painful Rocky Road
That we must cross and leave behind…
A difficult mountain to climb
Until we reach the clouds on the other side…
Have Faith…We will be united
We will be stronger, and we will SURVIVE…"

## I Saw a Little Angel Passing By
(Because of the pandemic)

I saw a little angel passing by,
Her face was pale, her hair was gold,
And in her little face, painted,
A little smile…

What happened to this little soul?
Someone blew off her flame of life
When it took this bud, before
It'll bloom into a flower, in her time…

Oh, how much pain it caused to see
The tears of parents in their agony.
To lose a part of them,
Gone!!! In this horrible tragedy…

Oh God, the pain it brought
To all the world to feel,
A violent act that brings forth sadness
In all this terrible misery…

All those little souls robbed of their lives
Bring to our eyes tears,
And breaks our hearts…
Leaving a feeling of impotence in our minds…

And there they went…among the clouds, up, into the sky,
And God gathered all into His arms,
Kiss them one by one, and, later let them go
To give birth to new angels in their flight…

*Susan Lidia Montes De Aragon*

# Betrayal

I'm emotionless, my soul is an empty cup
Of hopeful dreams for all my tomorrows.
An unpredictable and unjust lie of the loved one
Has taken me by surprise (I feel so much sorrow).

It suddenly fell in my aching heart
Like the sharp stroke of a falling knife;
(The one that betrayed me was the only one
That I could mostly trust...)

She knows that in the ashes of a broken marriage,
I fought to raise my three wild buds alone.
The burden was heavy in the struggle I carried,
But, persistence and survival made me go on...

She knew of my struggle, of my constant work
To see my children thru health, school, and sports.
She knew of my sleepless nights,
Of my tears when, because of them, the law called my door...

She knew of the court dates, of my comings and goings
To save them from horrible consequences up-front.
She knew of my trips to my son's college,
Of my tears when worried...

She knew that, when my son was intoxicated.
For him, his father's help I accepted,
Although I felt beaten and humiliated...
But, in spite of the truth, she lied and betrayed me...

I am the mother that raised them...

## Someone You Know?

Do you see that man
Walking down the road?
His face is dirty,
And dirty are his clothes…

His teeth are yellow,
His greasy hair long.
His eyes are red
From whiskey, I'm told…

Do you see him now?
Is he someone you know?

*Susan Lidia Montes De Aragon*

Bang!... Bang!...

It was sunset,
And the neighborhood gray.
The cry of a baby
A loud laughter breaks.
A few men came chatting
To the house of their friend;
A red Cadillac coming,
Cruising, and then...
The noise of the Bang!... Bang!...
A cloud of smoke makes,
And Bill's body fell...hanging
On the fence of his friend.
The shriek of the tires
As the Cadillac left.
The screams and the crying
As Bill's life comes to end,
And running was Sarah
When she saw Bill,
And screaming his mother
His body to see...
His friends were looking,
And looking at Bill.
His body was laying,
And laying so still.
They looked at each other
The next morning to swear:
(They have to pay
For the life of their friend).
"And Satan smiling
As he invited death..."

*We Are...A Bundle of Feelings and Emotions*

In Satan's arms falling
The souls of young boys
That desperate and lonely
The right path had lost,
And killing each other
They think they found the road
To eternity, or hell…brother…

Another day, and black moment,
The Bang!... Bang!... Again…

*Susan Lidia Montes De Aragon*

## The Wheel of Life

In a wheel of life we are only pursuing our closest dreams.
Some…in their search for money, others for their infinite dream of love.
But, our wishing doesn't seem to ever end.
For, when we think we finally reach it,
Whatever we wanted the most is never there,
And with a lasting hope of getting it tomorrow, we're always left…

Time passes us fast,
And with it, we say goodbye
To many dreams and happy illusions
That, with youth, we see passing by.
And we get new hopes
That brings us the sea of life,
With its constant rolling,
And its sweep away in a new tomorrow…

But, oh, that breathtaking spectacle of nature
Remains the same, who could have painted
Such landscape so perfectly?
Green plants moving slowly at the mercy of the playful wind,
And, while he blows, a symphony sings…
A strong tree of rich branches kissing rich earth,
While little flowers at her feet are at rest…

*We Are...A Bundle of Feelings and Emotions*

Those roses, gardenias, camellias,
Are blossoming perfections, here and there…
Improving our air, with all their scents…
I am holding a rose of red petals painted,
And, looking at it, I'm moved, created so perfectly,
It's delicate perfume reached my soul and my heart was taken…

Time passed and today, soon is tomorrow for us.
Outside is nature, unbelievable, untouched,—
To give us memories and beauty unmatched.
To give us peace and our spirits touch,
To give us new hope, and fill us with love…

*Susan Lidia Montes De Aragon*

# If

If I could ride on back of the rapids winds
And move everywhere.
To blow in every tormented soul: Peace.

If I could be an autumn leaf,
To fall and rise, and later fall again
Into an open wound: to heal.

If I could sing like a bird, day by day
To only sing everyone: A praise

If I could touch softly, like a feather,
And open all the flowers of the field.
To bring a smile in all the children's faces…

If I could be just like a cotton cloud,
To absorb all tears of sadness and doubt.

If I could spread on earth immense oceans of pure grain
To feed the world and stop the pain.

If I could be a giant butterfly
And spray my wings with magic love
To sprinkle tender sweetness all around.

Then, oh, how much pleasure I would find
If I could spread a blanket of happiness on everyone…

## The Turning of Time

Isn't it fast?
An instant short,
Before our hair turns silver,
The leaves to gold,
And our young bodies turn old…

Haven't you noticed?
Yesterday, today, tomorrow,
All seemed to go.
A fast moving day
From daylight to dawn.

And some things we couldn't finish yet,
Some good moments that past,
And we would like to still hold.
Because, all has gone too fast
From young to old…

And we still like to grasp
All those young beautiful moments
That are gone
Before the soft wind gently blows us
Away into the past.

Because, in our last breath,
We like to leave engraved
One more trace, of us…

*Susan Lidia Montes De Aragon*

Music

Music moves my soul and elevates it to the infinite.
Because music erases all the deep, sad emotions
That our heart keeps deep…

Music holds what I keep within.
Music resonates in the chambers of our hearts
When the notes keep playing
Caressing, echoing in my mind...

Without the soothing notes there is no peace;
It's like you are intertwined
In my body, within my being…

Don't stop, keep playing.
I need you to cheer me, embrace me, calm me,
With all the fast beats that make me dance,
And the soft sounds of violins that put me to sleep.

Play always, in all the places that destiny takes my life.
Never stop, keep playing,
Because I need you to survive
Until the end of me, and of my time…

## A Dancing Soul

And, when I died,
My spirit will fly away,
And fall into a dancing soul.
Because, as I experienced in life,
I know I cannot live without a song
To lift me up and fall into the happy waves,
And take me into a trance of happiness…

So please carry me away,
Hypnotise by the melodious sounds of every note,
And dancing, dancing, I will enter into an abyss…
Between the clouds I will peacefully float,
And dancing, softly
Into eternity I will go…

*Susan Lidia Montes De Aragon*

## My Life

Life is for me a constant struggle.
A fight to keep well all those around me.
All these frustrations keep my heart in a shadow
That embrace my soul with hopeless surroundings…

I'm tired of searching hard for happiness,
Only to end with empty hands and broken dreams,
And with waiting arms that extended
Waited for an empty space of love to be filled…

I feel like a broken, dry flower,
That is waiting in a garden to be picked;
That was moved and crushed in the endless struggle
To be loved, to be happy…but left again alone, in tears…

I cannot help but wonder
Is there a purpose for my life at all?
I closed my eyes many times and pondered,
How long like this?...How many days more?

## Destiny

Sometimes remembrances of happy moments
Sustain our spirits when passing thru painful periods of life.
Destiny moves us forward
Firmly holding our hands
And dragging us through
Difficult times awaiting us.
Because, in a instant, our fragile life can break
And we hope that, in our last breath
We will have enough time to say goodbye.
Because we are here now,
But maybe tomorrow will never come…

*Susan Lidia Montes De Aragon*

The End Is Coming…

The end is coming…I want to go fast,
Not linger on for a long time,
And bother those that take care of me.
Why should I take extra years of their lives
To take one more breath in an old, sickly body
That should rest, and say goodbye?
But, that's not in my hands,
Only God decides…

# Despair

See me…who aspired so much and got so little, yet smile,
See me…who dreamed great goals, soon to die.
See me…I'm only "despair" because of anxieties not told.
The one that some people tried to destroy
With disgusting gestures and lying words…

See me…I'm going slowly, everywhere I go,
Because I cannot achieve what my heart have told.
Everyone else occupied my deeds, invaded my mind.
And, meanwhile, the arms of my desperate soul have to cover its mouth…

*Susan Lidia Montes De Aragon*

## The Inevitable Surrender

The night is coming, like a thick rope falling
In the fields, on Earth, on all the flowers,
Cooling the warmth of daylight while the earth covering.
(The lights of hope in my heart slowly darkening…)

The last breath of my illusions dying.
I see all doors to a hopeful future closing.
All responsibilities to the old and young now surrounds me,
And escape I cannot from obligations that hold me…

The term of my life is becoming shorter.
My body and mind are suddenly aging;
It's the inevitable surrender and acceptance to becoming "older,"
It's nature, the normal span of life, that our "biological clock" is holding…

And I perceive that all those dreams that I fought so hard to reach
Are fading away intertwined with the mist of the night…
And I must kiss every wish of my unsatisfied heart "goodbye,"
To death give up…

## Destiny

I'm trying, very hard, with my ultimate and last spark of energy,
To move forward the pages of my fate.
Is this, all, going to end in an triumphant, wonderful ecstasy
Or in the shorten and sudden, expected coming of my death?

Many say that we can control our destiny,
And, with willpower, you can stop or change
The heavy arm of life that tends us to whip us,
But, no matter how hard we try, our life remains the same…

It is a major force that twist the road we follow,
Love that moves us or shakes us to bend,
Or change the plans that we so carefully started
Because something happened that we did not expect…

And we feel like dummies moved by destiny,
Pulled by the strings of our own, inevitable fate…

Another Chance

Over half my life gone.
I see, falling behind, a dull past.
(Like this day that dies, to be follow by the dawn)
And it is slowly fading in the obscure corners of my mind.

I don't see anyone next to me,
To be my close friend and give me comfort in the days to come.
I have no fortune to spend and to give me shelter
So in the winter, can help me to survive…

But there is still faith and hope holding me up
To give me happy dreams in lonely nights,
And feed my soul with expectations of delight…
And, it the turmoil of my life, because of my integrity,
I will have my pride to keep me fighting
Until the end of my determined time…

So, my advise, no matter what,
Don't ever give up.
Because, around the corner, you might encounter
Another chance…

## Enjoy

Enjoy, enjoy, enjoy
Before the darkness, like a curtain falls,
And takes away, in its arms,
Our lifeless souls…
The wind blows us away,
And, with the other leaves, we will roll and roll,
Somewhere in the infinite we'll go,
Becoming particles of this
And other worlds.
A lost shadow in the midst of all,
Or a floating light slowly moving away
Toward other lights that we'll join…

Where will our spirits go?
In light or darkness will we fall?
Are we going to be in pain
Or wonderful joy?
Are we going to re-live some day,
Or forever go?
Only God knows…

*Susan Lidia Montes De Aragon*

In Nature Soon to Be

As the pages are turning in the breeze of time,
And the inevitable beating of the constant tide
Are taking away slowly the grains of sand,
Our pulsating bodies are weakening until the end of life…
And in the water of the eternal sea
A little petal, my life, floating away, far away, I see;
Evaporating, intertwined between white bubbles and blue eternity.
Being one with nature, and in nature…soon to be…

## In an After Life

It is over…
With the last breath of my soul and
The last beating of my heart…
My body is aging fast
And, within myself, a guiding light
Is pushing my steps forward;
Meanwhile, a mirror is showing me
A sad picture of an old me
(After years beating my body to submission).
Soon, sickness and death will touch my soul,
And, taking me by the hand, will guide me
Away into the abyss,
And silence will follow a quiet goodbye…
All my hopes and dreams awaiting to be born,
Will be left behind…
"Maybe to be reborn again some day
In an after life…"

www.ingramcontent.com/pod-product-compliance
Lightning Source LLC
Chambersburg PA
CBHW020018050426
42450CB00005B/533